I0162453

It's a Mind Game

Separation, Divorce, and Starting Over

Bill Wagner

It's a Mind Game

copyright © 2024 Bill Wagner

ISBN: 978-1-959700-38-8

Bill Wagner

Dedication

To all my friends who helped me through
this time of my life.

Acknowledgments

Through the hardest of times, our Lord is always with us.

Preface

Bill was 42. It was his second divorce. The hopes of having a stable family into his retirement were being dashed. He had made mistakes. Bad choices, selfish choices, but he didn't think they were this bad. There was such a bond this time that seemed like it would last forever. It wasn't meant to be. For weeks after the separation and eventual divorce, Bill took to writing. Poems from the heart. Of what he was feeling. What he was experiencing. What the future looked like now. Not knowing whether to give up or struggle through. So many mixed emotions that at times would drive him to the brink of living. Someone had a plan. Years later, Bill found the love he had been searching for. This love would draw him closer to His Savior. This Savior was with him all through these trying times, but Bill wasn't looking for Him. He was looking for something he had lost again.

I hope that these poems help someone who is struggling through a divorce or separation.

There is one who is always with you. His name is Jesus. He will carry you through all of the hard times, hurtful times, unsure times. The ups and downs of the emotions that you will go through. Trust in Him and let the Spirit lead you.

Bill Wagner

Contents

Bill Wagner

Bill Wagner

Good Times

New places, new adventures shared,
Being with the ones who really cared.
Knowing now that you will survive,
Happy to be here, happy to be alive.

Knowing you have a place in the sun,
Forgetting the past, enjoying the present fun.
Seeing how much you did mature,
The wounds now healed, ready for a future.

The choices now made without a doubt,
Makes you confident, makes you shout.
So many good times now to be had,
Releasing the memories of feeling sad.

Friends that have been so near,
Being there for me without any fear.
Our future now looks so bright,
At the end of the tunnel, there is a light.

Triangle

Can't be with the one you love,
So, love the one you are with.
It seems so very easy to do.
Is it a curse or a gift?

A heart that longs to give love,
Shows it to the one that is near.
So easy to say three little words,
But which one is true love, the other, fear?

Being alone has lasted too long,
Never been like this, so afraid.
The fear of this being this way always,
A tender touch, a tender word, never said.

Never say never, it will come true,
Some of what has happened is so wrong.
If they find out what has been done,
Most will leave, it will all be gone.

Keep my silence, keep the secret within,
Not wanting to give or receive hurt no more.
What I'm doing should never have been,
Lock up my heart, close shut the door.

Bill Wagner

She Can't Let Go

Reaching out to hold my hand,
A true friend in this troubled land.
Her independence and freedom she wants,
She has it now, but the memory haunts.

Can't let go of what she had,
The life she left wasn't so bad.
Now, she's out there all alone,
With the fear of it all gone.

Trying to hold onto a precious gift,
How her children gave her a lift.
But so many times they're not there,
Like the days she left them, who cared?

With pen in hand, it may be the last
Hold she has to keeping the past.
With this new life, she had hoped to find,
Bring the reality of life lost, so unkind.

In My Heart

I can't show you how I feel,
My love for you is all too real.
There's still a pain in my heart,
It still hurts that we are apart.

So easy, at times, to show my love,
That it's true, as from above.
I want to reach out so desperately,
But I'm so afraid you'll hurt me.

There's such a love for you inside,
It's all I can do to let it hide.
Sometimes I don't think you understand,
Just what you really mean to this man.

The trust I had for you isn't there,
Being so afraid that you can't be here.
To give the love we so desperately need,
That you'll be selfish, full of greed.

No matter what I do or don't say,
No matter what may happen today.
A new life we want to start,
You will always be there, in my heart.

Bill Wagner

The Game

The love we have for the game,
Through the years has stayed the same.
The desire within us is born,
Away from our family that was torn.

The intensity we feel inside,
The excitement is hard to hide.
Upon our face is a silly grin,
With the hopes we will win.

The comradery we will share,
How the game is played shows we care.
It doesn't matter what they are paid,
Is the team intact? Who has stayed?

Yes, this game gives us such a thrill,
Today, tomorrow, it always will.
In our kids, the legacy lives on,
Long, long after we are gone.

Return

Waking up with you by my side,
The pain and hurt, you can't hide.
The past again has made a return,
Awaking emotions that still burn.

Your new love's bringing you pain,
Disrupting our lives again.
Leave us alone is all I ask,
Has this been too hard a task?

Today, I wanted to say, "I told you so."
But my love for you won't let it go.
The hurt that you feel
Shows what you had was so real.

The fear I have, the lack of trust,
You can't come home— it hurts too much.
Though my heart for you does yearn,
We can't, for now, let you return.

Bill Wagner

Dancing

With good friends, feeling at ease,
Not having anyone to please.
Not having to take any chances,
Just get on the floor and do the dances.

The frustration, the stress, goes away.
Moving to the music, feeling the body sway.
Getting lost with the good times,
Knowing your light still shines.

So many people out on the floor,
But you're good, you won't be a bore.
You've tried so hard to reach the top,
You hope this feeling will not stop.

Not looking for love or any romancing.
All you want is the music and dancing.
Your feet make you feel so light,
Holding onto this with all your might.

Don't Fall Down

Don't let her in again with her pain,
You've finally gotten in out of the rain.
No matter what is there inside,
Keep it locked up, let it hide.

If you fall now, everything will be lost.
Don't fall down at any cost.
A friend now is all you can be.
You've got to be strong, can't you see?

You've both been out running around,
Taking in the sights, burning up the town.
You've taken hold of your life,
Walked away from the pain and strife.

Keep your emotions to yourself,
Hide them away, put them on the shelf.
Keep them quiet, not making a sound,
Whatever you do, don't fall down.

Bill Wagner

Again

Again I played the fool,
Couldn't control my emotions, wasn't cool.
And now it tears at my little girl's heart,
She is confused, torn apart.

My love for her, I can't hide,
The hurt she gives me tears me inside.
I thought there was a chance to win
Her love for me, she would let me in.

My foolish pride, I did show,
Couldn't keep quiet, wouldn't let it go.
When will my love for her die?
When will I stop wanting to cry?

I want her so bad, back in my life.
I want her home, I miss my wife.
Things will never be like it had been,
I just hope I won't be a fool again.

True Love

What is true love?
A blessing or a curse from above?
Though all the hurt and pain you feel,
You try to show your love is real.

Everything you show is all in vain,
Everything lost, nothing to gain.
You try to grab the brass ring,
Feel the joy, to have your heart sing.

And just when you feel that you are there,
Your world falls apart without a care.
If your love is real, let it go,
If it is true, you will know.

She's been back, she says she loves me.
Is it real or is she just lonely?
Since she went away, I'm alone.
I've shown others love unlike she's known.

Can I ever have true love again?
Not if it brings this much rain.
Do I want to have a new love?
No, not even it it's on the wings of a dove.

Bill Wagner

A Candle Still Burns

The flicker of the flame still burns,
A warmth in the room, still yearns.
The darkness it fights to keep away,
Chasing away the fears, till the light of day.

It started out so tall and strong,
The battles it fought, trying to right a wrong.
How it does shimmer when the winds blow,
The feelings it has, no one knows.

With a hope it never goes out,
Does anyone know what it's all about?
As our separate lives go on,
A candle still burns with a love its own.

I Can't Leave You

All the years, I felt so secure.
Our love lasting forever, I felt so sure.
The plans for our future so bright.
Being together felt so right.

Now I'm fighting back all the emotions.
The waves tossing my heart like an ocean.
I'm not supposed to love you anymore,
It didn't go with you out the door.

It still seems like yesterday you were here.
Now, no more trust, too much fear.
I can't leave you with a bad goodbye,
Never meaning to hurt or make you cry.

We're fighting now, the love of a little girl,
If we don't watch, we'll destroy her world.
Maybe I try to hold onto a piece of you,
There's not much more I can do.

No matter what I say or do,
My heart just won't leave you.
You have such a strong hold on me,
My love, strong for you, will always be.

Bill Wagner

My Writing

It seems the only time I can write
Is when someone isn't holding me tight.
When the emptiness within me flows,
The light is out, no longer glows.

The reason for writing is always the same:
I'm still hurting, I'm in too much pain.
And so many times, as I often do,
I wonder, do you feel this emptiness, too?

Your talent was always in your art.
How can anyone draw, paint a broken heart?
Is the canvas enough to draw a river of tears,
Can you make the shadows show our fear?

When I write, I write from my heart,
Can they see and hear what it's like apart?
With pen in hand I write what I feel,
With the brush, can you make it real?

I don't know if this is a blessing or curse.
I know sometimes, it does get worse.
Writing helps me ease my pain,
Everything to lose and everything to gain.

Today

Today my love and I,
Talked about the future, I cry.
So much doubt within,
Where to start, where to begin.

What has happened brings fears,
A lot of sorrow, a lot of tears.
But what do we know?
Quit worrying, let love grow.

We talk of my past.
My loves that didn't last.
Of not being able to understand,
The problems now at hand.

The thing that amazes me,
The heartaches ahead she can't see.
No matter that this is wrong,
Her love for me was so strong.

I know in time, it will last.
Look towards the future, forget the past.
Today, she gave me all the reason,
To live for now, live for the season.

Bill Wagner

Picking up the Pieces

The time it takes to build a dream,
Vanished in a heartbeat, or so it seems.
A life built together, the vows made,
Has turned into anger and so much rage.

Two people so happy in love,
Blessed this union from above.
Into this life, new lives were brought,
Now, all is gone, a lesson taught.

A home, cars, furniture to bring us comfort,
Pile it all together, out of it, we'll sort.
Tearing at the memories, I'll take this or that
But give it here, that's my hat.

Who gets the kids? Who'll pay the bills?
Keeping emotions in check, a test of wills.
The love has died, our togetherness ceases,
Life goes on now, picking up the pieces.

Blind Date

A friend of a friend, is all it took,
At a glance, just one look.
Who would know what tonight may bring,
How she would make my heart sing.

The tenderness of her touch, feel of her hair,
Made the world go away, I didn't care.
We danced the night away,
Tonight with me, she would stay.

How could we tell the happiness we shared,
No more loneliness, we've been spared.
The next few days have been a joy,
We felt like kids with a new toy.

The honesty I feel with her,
No more of the way things were.
She feels so good in my arms,
To keep her safe, free from harm.

We've had so much pain in our life,
From her husband, from my wife.
Because of fear, I still hesitate,
But look what I found, this blind date.

Bill Wagner

Her Song

The tenderness, the passion she shows,
Inside her so much love grows.
The pain she has felt is in the past,
She hopes that this will last.

She has told so many how she feels,
That finding a good man is so real.
A love, she thought, had died,
It wasn't because she hadn't tried.

Now, the tenderness she feels inside,
A love, a happiness, she cannot hide.
She told this man there'll be no strings,
Just listen to how her heart sings.

The happiness she has felt
With him, her heart does melt.
The laughter that her children can see,
Can come out now, so let it be.

I want to take her hand, keep her warm,
Take her away from all of life's harm.
Vows to her wouldn't feel like a duty,
It would be such an honor, Tooty.

Missed Chances

A time when you reached out, held my hand,
I needed a friend in this troubled land.
The past few months we've grown so close,
In a short time, you'll be a ghost.

Gone to a better place, to start a new life,
You'll soon become a lucky man's wife.
The last time I saw you, I could only stare,
Looking at the two of you, joy filled the air.

We've found out too late, we let it slip away,
A love that, through our silence, gone today.
The memories we shared the most,
In a few short days will all be lost.

Take care my dear, in your search you find
The happiness so well deserved, is so kind.
The sound of your voice, the taste of a kiss,
The way we touched, all of this I will miss.

No more will I be able to call your name,
Your lost love, I have me to blame.
Someday our path will cross in passing cars,
Who knows, the 'Keeper of the Stars'?

Bill Wagner

Mother

I know that I will never be,
The son you're proud to those to see.
So many times there has been pain,
But it has been honesty, not shame.

We are two that say what we feel,
It's our heritage that makes it real.
We keep secrets to protect those we love,
Many don't understand, only Him above.

Times have caused us not to be there,
When we need each other, but we still care.
Though we seldom show a tender hand,
It's what's happened to us, understand.

We do try to do what is best,
Not only for us, but for all the rest.
Like us, there'll be no other,
I very seldom tell you, "I love you, Mother."

Breathless

I know how I feel, it scares me to death,
Being with her just takes my breath.
The way everyone has accepted me,
Us being together, it's just too easy.

Being with her just seems so natural,
And when I'm away from her, I'll call.
Sometimes I want to be by her side,
I can't be, I have too much to hide.

An affair from which I can't walk away,
I have gotten in too deep, too much to pay.
I wish this hadn't gone so far,
Maybe I need to wish upon a star.

She wants this to be so much more,
I can't, somehow I've got to close the door.
Every time I hold this new love tight,
I could say I love you. Someday I might.

What do ya do when this love comes along,
Can this be it, or just another song?
Someday I'll get out of this mess,
All I know now is she leaves me breathless.

Bill Wagner

True to Form

The day you left us, we were on our own,
As time has passed, we should have known.
To depend on you, was a fantasy,
The kids and me, all there were, or will be.

To think that you really care,
How can you, when you aren't there?
When we get to talk, I get the blame,
But it's you, Dear, that lives with the shame.

Maybe someday our lives will turn around.
Maybe you'll have a life, way across town.
But now it's a struggle to provide,
These kids with their needs. I hurt inside.

You say what I do will affect the kids.
It's not what I say or do, but what you did.
Sometimes we wish we weren't borne,
But I'll stay the same, you'll be true to form.

Don't Close Your Eyes

Don't close your eyes, you'll wake up soon
To a world of reality, a very different tune.
You've lived in a world of make believe.
When the sun comes up, you will grieve.

Gone is the world of security and hope,
Not one of loud music, drink, and dope.
A world of love from husband and children,
Just when our life was starting to begin.

Don't close your eyes, you'll lose your need,
Being too selfish, filled with so much greed.
Thinking only of yourself and not of others,
Happiness will end, a life gets smothered.

When you close your eyes, you'll still see,
What you did to us, what you did to me.
Like the darkness that fills the skies,
A world that is dark, don't close your eyes.

Bill Wagner

A Father/Mother I Can't Be

A mother and father, I can't be,
All of this is so new to me.
Everything, good or bad, I'm to blame,
Whatever happens, I bear the shame.

What does it take to make a home?
When you're trying it alone.
I know it will take time to get it right,
I get so tired by the time it's night.

Maybe they should go to mother.
Then I wouldn't be here to be a bother.
Go somewhere else they can take pride,
Where they won't be so ashamed inside.

So, heartless they can sometimes be,
They don't realize how hard it is on me.
If they could understand, it will be fine.
I'll get it right, it just takes time.

Not Yet Gone

Tonight I once again spoke her name,
The sound of her voice, still the same.
A time when we once were so close,
I guess I still love her ghost.

A new life she's trying to lead,
What he gives is what she needs.
It seems she is now so happy,
I hope it is what she wants it to be.

I missed my chance to be by her side,
The feelings I had, I kept inside.
An old love, a new life, a new home,
But in my heart, she's not gone.

She's not yet gone, I have her memory,
Of a love we wouldn't let be.
Someday maybe, she'll be home.
In my heart, she's not yet gone.

Bill Wagner

Little Girl Grown

Shirley Temple curls, auburn hair,
Smile on her face, not a care.
Baby shoes, little sundresses,
Barbie's her favorite, she makes messes.

A tender heart she gets from both of us,
She knows not a stranger, has a gentle touch.
She's always happy, even playing with dirt,
But sometimes she is so easily hurt.

She loves her mother, she doesn't want pain,
Wishes mom would come out of the rain.
She misses her so, wishes she didn't go,
Seeing her puts her little heart aglow.

And now she's ready for her first dance,
Which little boy will get the chance?
Our little girl, where has she gone?
Now she looks like our little girl grown.

Scared

The loneliness surrounds my world,
The night has become my enemy.
Emptiness has filled my life,
I'd trade it all to not be alone.

When I had someone, I took for granted
They're gone, so much pain.
What keeps me alone is the fear.
Fear of the hurt I don't want to face.

Built a wall around my love,
Won't let anyone in.
Fighting so desperately to let it out,
Shouting, pleading for the freedom.

Someday my wish will come true,
I'll be touched by love again.
The kind I so desperately need,
Until then, I'm scared.

Bill Wagner

YOU

You came into my life from nowhere,
A smile on your face, didn't have a care.
In this short time, we've gotten so close,
So close, maybe too close, no one knows.

You know everything I say and do,
No one knows me as well as you.
You're the only one to see me cry,
Always there, always by my side.

You would always tell me how you feel,
If it was a fantasy, or if it was real.
And somewhere along the way, you get lost,
Everything you wanted was at a cost.

You're the one whose problems are so deep,
The confusion inside of you was so steep.
It was me who brought it to a head,
It was me whose deserted you instead.

You accepted me for what I am,
No matter the hurt, as only you can.
My thoughts are of you every day,
It doesn't matter what I say. I miss you.

Go Away

The pain I feel so deep inside,
Time has let me learn how to hide.
Your actions all run so true.
I know you completely, I do.

I can tell when you start to run,
You came around and I don't show fun.
How I feel for you has you so afraid,
What am I supposed to do? What's to say?

Telling you I love you and miss you,
I don't cover up well like you do.
The pity I feel for you for what you hide,
Not showing what you feel, not even tried.

Someday you will have let this slip by,
When you sit alone and all you do is cry.
Empty walls and loneliness each day.
You can't come home, just go away.

Bill Wagner

Can't be Friends

We thought we had something unique,
Friendship amidst turmoil, at a peak.
No, the high is gone,
I don't want to ever hear your song.

I can't be your friend like you wish,
It's your touch, it's you I miss.
Sometimes it's been so hard
I can't do this no more. I'm tired.

My love to you was all I wanted,
You in my life, it was haunted.
Couldn't let myself feel love anymore,
Without someone in my life, life's a bore.

Someday I will be just your friend,
You won't run from me again.
But what you'll feel will be hurt,
The loss we will suffer. What's it worth?

Youth

Growing up is so hard to do,
Even though you already think so.
The responsibility can come so easy,
If it fits your schedule that's so busy.

I know I make it hard sometimes,
But I don't want your life to be like mine.
It's tough to be all grown up,
The taste is bitter from the cup.

I want so much better for you,
I only guide you on what to do.
Some day you will be able to see,
Then you will want to thank me.

Till that day comes, we'll make the best
Of a crazy life. What a mess!
You will open up to the truth,
Your future lies ahead, O youth.

Bill Wagner

A Bond Broken

Words of anger, words of pain.
A love that will never be again.
What once was right is now wrong
What used to be is now completely gone.

A love, a life to die for.
A memory, like the closing of a door.
What was said can't be taken back
It was stretched too far, given into the attack

Wishing it hadn't but knowing it would
Be better but it never could.
All the times there was no one but us
Now we look at each other and cuss.

We stop short of calling out names.
It went too far, too long, it wasn't a game.
No matter now, how much we differ
It's our children that will suffer.

The pain and anger they feel inside
They learnt too soon how to hide.
No more tender words will be spoken
Our love is gone, the bond broken.

Used to Be

The way my life has begun to change
So familiar, yet so strange.
The security I feel at home
Content to be here, not to roam.

The love of my life is now a hate
Being alone has taught me to wait.
My friends and I have gotten so close
Knowing that helps the most

Having fun like I use to
Chases away the mood, so blue
Someone that I know who loves me.
Someday, together we will be.

I'll make it in this life
Amid the turmoil and the strife.
I haven't forgotten my Father above,
His forgiveness and wonderful love.

Without God in your life, it's meaningless.
Without His guidance, you'll be in a mess.
I've got to return to Him, yes indeed,
He is all we really need.

Bill Wagner

Distant Drums

The sound of beating so far away
Two hearts that once were one, one day.
Two hearts that knew each other's need.
Two lives that were one, indeed.

Drums that beat in harmony.
A love for only you and me.
Drums with a beautiful beat
Sounded as one when our eyes did meet.

The something happened, we lost the sound,
The music quit, it hit the ground.
We started playing to a different beat.
No longer one, we're on a different sheet.

What happened, no one is sure.
It just left— a love so pure.
The beat still so far away
Still calls to each other for one more day.

Sometimes now, the sound is so strong
Deceiving us, saying the sound isn't wrong.
Too much distance now without the sun.
All the beats now is a lonely distant drum.

Newbie

With eyes so full of life,
Who knows she's full of strife.
The bounce she has in her step
Hiding the times she sat and wept.

My heart jumps to see her face.
Could I ever find a place?
A place inside a broken heart
So filled with fear, so dark.

Take my hand, sunshine eyes.
Let me love you, don't deny.
Be patient, it takes time to mend.
You have to be my lover, my friend

I watch your face at somewhere new
Like a kid with a new toy, this is you.
A new life that is so different.
I wonder where the innocence went.

Bill Wagner

When the Honeymoon's Over

A time when you want to roll in clover
When you never think a love is over
To touch each other, your heart does swoon.
You can touch the stars, jump over the moon

A kiss that sets off fireworks.
Overlooking each other's little quirks.
Out in public, still holding hands,
Working together to meet life's demands.

Sitting in the quiet, talking about the future
Holding each other, a love to still nurture.
Making plans for when we're old,
Our love would keep us out of the cold.

What happened next, no one knows.
An ill wind came, a cold wind blows.
No longer wanting to hold my hand,
Not wanting to be together in this land.

The longing for each other is long gone.
The words we say now cut to the bone.
Can't stand each other, we run for cover.
Life's so unsure, the honeymoon's over.

Too Many Loves

An old love that I am without.
A new love filled with so much doubt.
Another love on a different level.
Yet another love, that's scary, you devil.

Too many loves, kept apart.
But, sometimes not enough, a lonely heart.
To none can I be true.
I try so hard, until I'm blue.

Giving into this loneliness
Creating such a nasty mess.
Each love, I can't walk away
For fear of being alone today.

I know someday I'll take the fall.
Loose each one, Loose them all.
It's strange, for I once had just one.
I thought my life had just begun.

Then suddenly, it all came to an end,
These new loves, I can't be just a friend,
It's all or nothing, so it would seem,
I try not to hurt them or be mean.

Bill Wagner

So, today, which one or ones do I love?
Sometimes, I ask for guidance from above.
I wish I could love just once again.
How could I live so much in sin?

Trapped

I wrote of her a long time ago,
Of a time when she felt so low.
I watched her change for the better.
Thanking God for the day I met her.

I've seen her happy, I've seen her pain.
She felt good about herself once again.
Looking forward to a new life to have.
Making the best of a marriage to save.

Little did we know how she felt,
That a tender touch, her heart would melt
She got closer than what we thought.
She fell for a friend with a tender touch.

And though this love was so one sided,
She had tried so hard to just hide it.
So afraid the love would run away
Hoping him to be hers one day.

But life can be so very cruel
Her marriage had turned into a duel
Now, she's again trapped inside the walls.
Can't go out, see no one, just walk the halls.

Bill Wagner

So sorry, it's all my fault.
The love for him was all for naught.
She's been threatened not to leave.
She'll stay at home, she will grieve.

Freedom

When our forefathers wanted to be free,
They fought and died for their country.
For their independence they would die.
A supreme sacrifice, but they wanted to try.

You wanted freedom, but little did you know
That there was a sacrifice in the shadow.
To have freedom and independence is nice
But to get that, there is a price.

When it felt like you had it all,
You had a great time, until it began to fall.
Apart is what it's doing now.
You got lonesome, you miss it. Wow!

Was the freedom worth the pain.
I know that I am the one to blame.
Until the day comes that you realize
What you got, what you have, is the prize.

You wanted it all, hoping we'll be there.
Selfishness is what you showed, didn't care.
I haven't got what I wanted, can't you see?
A family, a marriage, but couldn't let it be.

Bill Wagner

Everyone now gets the blame.
But it's you who should bear the shame.
Back to us, you wouldn't come.
What's the price of your freedom?

Lead You On

You want me to say, I miss you so.
Something from me that I can't show.
What you want for you may be real.
For me, it's not the same that I feel.

I enjoy the good times we have.
The times together, the love-making we save
But to love you, I cannot.
What's between us is not that hot,

You are not constantly on my mind.
That kind of love, I'm trying to find.
At one time, I had it all
Then I took a very hard fall.

I got a strong dose of reality.
I found out what true love meant to me.
Using you is not what it's meant to be.
No one understands, can't you see?

Tell me good-bye, it's the best for you.
I will only hurt you, not meaning to.
In so many ways, I have grown.
I owe it to you, but I'll still lead you on.

Bill Wagner

Keep the Fire Burning

Such an emptiness inside me.
An emptiness that only you could fill.
Once a love that was so complete.
A lifetime together was so real.

It's been some time since you went away.
I've grown to accept this loneliness.
A coldness has filled a once warm heart
Not letting anyone answer my distress.

So many loves to try to replace
The love you had, but you gave away.
I reach out in so many directions
In hopes to fill this void one day.

I ask you for my freedom, a chance
That by being free I can stop this yearning
To have the love that was once ours,
To stop the fire that is burning.

Out of the Past

A tenderness that is missed.
A memory of lips I kissed.
The touching of my heart as you did.
What I do now, I dread.

Involvement with someone I can't leave.
What was lost, I miss, I grieve.
The happiness around me once did abound.
Now my life was falling to the ground.

The family that made my heart soar
Won't be with me, I'm a bore.
Reaching out to have someone at last.
How can they come from my past?

Two loves that were held so dear.
With each one, there's so much fear.
I tried to give them my love.
Maybe it was too tight like hand and glove.

I miss them and they miss me.
Maybe I should just let it be.
Whatever happens, don't go too fast.
Heartache can also come out of the past.

Bill Wagner

A Time to Let Go

A time to let go of a love that can't be.
The hope of rekindling a strong unity.
We tried and alas, we failed.
Our boat together will never have sailed.

I'm not sure if there are no regrets.
There are things we both just couldn't get.
It wasn't so much a lack of love,
The loss of trust and the push to shove.

My wife of seventeen years
Was lost in a river of tears.
What caused us both to change?
I stop and think that it's so strange.

What has happened to this family
In the last few months, it can never be.
It's a shame, but we'll never know.
Now it's just a time to let it all go.

Starting over is all we can do.
Time itself, all the pain, will undo.
What happens now only God above knows.
Hold onto what we have, hope it grows.

At a Distance

At a distance, I watched you grieve.
A death had happened, 'twas hard to believe.
Someone else held your heart.
When we needed someone, we're still apart.

You say there's really no one there.
But with me, you say you care.
The answer is always the same,
No one's here, I can't call your name.

When I tell you how I feel,
You don't want to talk, the talk you'll kill.
A part of your family I can't be.
Someone's taken my place, can't you see?

And now someone's messing up your life.
Calling my friends, saying they're my wife.
I've asked you, but you said no.
I have trouble believing this is so.

I'm at a distance, though I don't want to be
But that's where you feel safe with me.
You won't let me close because of the fear
Of not being sure of my love, my dear.

Bill Wagner

Looking

Out into the darkness I stare.
Is there anyone who will care?
To reach out and hold this empty soul
Before the emptiness takes its toll.

Searching throughout the night for one
Who'll help me find the sun.
Cast me out of this Dungeon of Heartache
To prove that to love is no mistake.

Is there someone out there to lend a hand?
To share my life within this troubled land.
To bring the joy that once filled my life.
Who doesn't bring the hurt, cut like a knife?

If I can only find the one to share my pain,
I'll do my best to chase away the rain.
I will show my love with more than touch.
Give me someone, I only ask this much.

Questions

You read the things that I write
Wondering if what you read is right.
The words that I write are from the heart.
They're from a love grown apart.

I tried to make you see what I feel.
The feelings I show are not now real.
They're of a time that has long past
Of two lives that were not meant to last.

The pain that's in the words you read
Were of a lonely man in need.
A need of someone to help warm the night
Who tries to survive with all his might.

A man who has such a great fear inside,
Who won't open up because of hurt pride.
Who fears again that he will fail.
Look at his past, it tells the tale.

So many nights this man spends alone.
No one there to call his own.
Always there was someone in his life.
Now, no one to help through the strife.

Bill Wagner

So, don't read a lot into these lines
Because someday his light again will shine.
One to fill his heart to chase the pain
Who will let him live and love again.

Where Are You Now?

You go a few days without a sound,
Then you show up, you come around.
You show that you really care.
When all of a sudden, you're not there.

How can anyone get so close
When you act like a ghost?
Are you hurting so much inside
That all you want is to come in and hide?

There was a time when we needed you so
But you wouldn't come around, on the go.
Now it's us that can't sit still.
A family together has lost its thrill.

Time, they say, will heal it all.
In the meantime, we continue to fall.
A thousand miles would seem so much.
Where are you now? Where is your touch?

Bill Wagner

Is it Better Now?

Almost two years since you've been gone.
It's not so bad now, being alone.
Somehow I've learned to adjust.
It wasn't necessary, but a must.

For so many years you were there.
Someone to hold, to care.
There has been several trying to replace,
But so far, no one can stand the pace.

The ups and downs, my ins and outs,
My quiet times, my time to shout.
Too many out there more messed up than me
They can't understand, they can't see.

There is one who holds a special place,
But It can't be, too much space.
Is it better now, this life of mine.
Only one thing can tell it's time.

Many ways, my emotions I control.
But in many ways, the pain has taken its toll.

How Long

How long before you decide?
A love you can no longer hide.
How long will I have to be alone?
What will it take for you to be gone?

It's been a long time since your plan.
Why haven't you completed, if you can?
Is this what you really want to do?
Who knows any more, it's up to you.

The choice to be made is yours,
To keep them open or close the doors.
The decision is yours to make.
It's your chance, you have to take.

Live the life that you're now in.
If I hurt you, I ask to be forgiven.
This waiting game, how long does it last?
How long before we're a thing of the past?

Bill Wagner

Again, Again

The loneliness won over again.
I told her that I missed her so.
Of how I had hoped to have seen,
Seen her this weekend, it was a dream.

I miss her by my side, holding on.
Feeling that every battle won.
Starting over is so hard to do.
Making a new life without you.

It's just an emotion, I know.
The pain of forever letting go.
Make a date, hold her hand,
Letting my heart take command.

Somehow, some way, I can't go through
With all the feelings of missing you.
Marching on, making a new life,
Moving amongst all the strife.

If there were someone here at my side,
My feelings for you would be easy to hide.
But the loneliness brings the rain.
And here I am, missing you again.

Be Strong

All my life, it meant to me
To have a home, a job, a family.
What happened, what went wrong?
Now I'm alone, I have to be strong.

All my dreams have been shattered.
What does it mean, what does it matter?
What caused our life to go astray?
I ask this question almost every day.

The lonely nights I must now face
Doing as one not two, what a pace.
The emptiness where you once belong.
Can't worry now, I have to be strong.

What happened to the one by my side?
Which one failed, which one tried?
So many questions without answers.
Was it my fault, or was it hers?

It doesn't matter, we can't place the blame.
A life together now gone, what a shame.
I hear, every day, in the words of a song,
"Help me make it, let me be strong."

Bill Wagner

Make Questions

We talk on the phone.
When we can be alone.
Two hearts beating the same.
Is it love or a game?

Scared to death but wanting it so.
Times shared together, hearts aglow.
A love so desperately needed.
With open arms, we are greeted.

So easy, too easy, to show that we care.
Hurt too much in a life out there.
We know each other, we need
Not for sex, money, or greed.

Companionship, someone to be true.
To mean it when told, I love you.
A love to last the rest of our life.
Not sure if it should be husband and wife.

So Afraid

The love you say you have for me
Terrifies me. I'm afraid to let it be.
You don't know what it is I feel,
But the loneliness is so real.

I can't wait to hold you so tight.
Also afraid that you will take flight.
I want so much to let it be
So you know what it is to be lonely.

I've adjusted to a life without someone
To hold me, to undo what life has done.
I still live with a memory
Of a love lost, of what it used to be.

Can you accept the way that I feel?
The fear, the pain that can kill,
Can kill the chance of a love so true.
Can you ever understand, can you?

In such a short time, we've gotten so close.
Can you live with a ghost?
I want you in my arms so tight.
I'm afraid I can't hold you tonight.

Bill Wagner

The longer I go, the less I want to be
With someone; so afraid, can't you see?
I don't think you understand
What has happened to this man.

What Happened?

When in life a tender word is spoken,
The wrong words said, a heart broken.
A life that could begin anew
Becomes a recluse, hidden from view.

Tender words so filled the heart.
What happened, when did it part?
Who's to blame, whose is at fault?
Years together, all for naught.

The vows made to God above.
Forever together, undying love.
Keeping from the children all the pain.
Here comes the clouds. Where is the rain?

Take my hand, walk with me.
I hate you, you S.O.B.
Tender words, now long gone.
A broken family, a broken home.

Where do they all go from here ?
New beginnings and a new fear.
Starting over is so hard to do.
Who's at fault, me or you?

Bill Wagner

Where Do I Go From Here?

Gone is the new love I found.
Walked away, couldn't stay around.
Messed up in the head from loneliness.
Everything I do is second-guessed.

Why take a chance on love anymore?
I'd just end up walking out the door.
I just can't seem to forget
The love of my life who up and went.

I have someone who is special to me.
It seems our lives are in harmony.
I wish we were together
But like before, there is another.

So where do I go from here.
I run up front but fall to the rear.
Day to day life I begin to dread.
All this messes up my head.

The loneliness I can't stand no more.
Being without someone is a total bore.
In love, in life, it's failing that I fear.
So, where do I go from here?

71

Walking Away

Walking away from a love
Knowing it was so true.
Too much pain, too much hassle,
Really not knowing what to do.

A love that should have never been.
Sometimes it seemed like a game
Waiting for the right time.
The answer was always the same.

The best of both worlds it did seem
Having one for home and money.
The other out on a string
I want you to make love to me, Honey.

Walking away, maybe the best thing to do.
Away from the scheduled calling
And the scheduled rendezvous.

Take my hand and walk with me.
Not until he's the one to leave.
You said you wanted to hold my hand.
Walking away, we both do grieve.

Bill Wagner

She Cried

When the love she had searched for,
The feeling of being ignored,
The happiness she tried so hard to find
Had worked against her heart and mind.

I never knew how hard she tried
Until that night with me she cried.
I hadn't known her very long
But I know where her heart did belong.

With a man for whom she shared for years
That night she cried a river of tears.
A man from whom she just needed attention.
Being with her, doing with her, no mention.

Career, family, she gave her devotion.
A new life, love of life, she set into motion.
This man she loved so very much
Had forgotten, did he know, a tender touch.

She would want him night or day.
Rejection, all she got, all he would say.
After a while, her heart got lonely.
She didn't want to be with her one and only.

Someone Wanted

Someone to give me peace of mind
Whose love I know is true
Who will stand by my side
In everything that I do.

Someone in this life
Who will be my friend
Who knows me inside out
Upon whom I can depend.

Someone not looking for the perfect man,
With me they will be content.
Full of passion and desire
That I won't ask where it went.

Someone who makes me feel so secure
Knowing that's where they want to be.
With each other we'll find strength.
Not once, wanting to be free.

Bill Wagner

Dad

There once was a time I wanted to be
Like this man. Every day I would see,
Trying so hard for his approval.
Always trying, forever futile.

Wishing I could make him proud.
He would call out my name so loud.
Through two marriages lost, I tried so hard.
How could I know life would be marred?

His hurt was all I could bear.
Tired of him not being there.
No more trying to be
With him, what I couldn't make him see.

Now, in my solitude, I will stand
Without my family to lend a helping hand.
You know it really is sad
To live a life alone without your Dad.

In the Moonlight

In the moonlight, her beauty did shine.
The look on her face told me she was mine.
The twinkling of the stars could be found
In the sparkling of her eyes, not a sound.

A tenderness I thought was gone,
I felt I wouldn't be left alone.
Her arms around me, I feel so secure.
Having her love, I know for sure.

No more lonely, lonely night
For she'll be there to hold me tight.
Her love makes me feel so warm.
A new love, my heart, safe from harm.

Bill Wagner

Fair-Weather Friend

A fair-weather friend I'm not.
I'll be there when you're in a spot.
When you need me, I'll be there.
I'm your friend, I really care.

Don't ignore me when you're arm in arm,
Someone new, can he keep you from harm?
When we're out for everyone to see,
Don't act like you don't know me.

When you feel the need to be held,
My friendship for you will never yield.
Don't reach out to someone to hold
When your arms have been so cold.

If of me you're not ashamed,
I'm at fault, the one to be blamed.
For showing someone I care
When they read something that isn't there.

If this is all you think of me,
Just tell me so, hear my plea.
If with you there is so much doubt.
I'll walk away, friendship you'll be without.

Lonely is the Lost Love

She lashes out at me again.
She can only stand so much pain,
Maybe I'm wrong to take a stand.
Too many times I gave a tender hand.

My life is still such a mess.
I need someone, a tender caress.
Maybe it's the security that I feel.
My living alone, the emotion it did kill.

I don't feel the sorrow that was there.
When we argued, it was her who didn't care.
I guess time has hardened my heart.
Too much time, me and the kids, apart.

It's still me who gets the blame.
It's still me who feels the shame.
In her own way, she still needs me.
Afraid to tell the truth, she lets it be.

If God will spare her, to withstand the test,
I know she will succeed, do her best.
For so long, I only wanted her to see
There was enough love for her and me.

Bill Wagner

But now she's in a world of her own.
Dealing with emotions she's never known.
Hard to keep living, day by day, it's a must.
She doesn't know this family she can trust.

I Can't Believe

I can't believe what's happened to me.
The family we had, had to leave.
All year long, there has been so much doubt.
The life we once had, now we're without.

Our new year has been the same.
She's not here, we can't call her name.
Why can't this woman see
Our love to give to her, it can't be?

Friends have told me they didn't know
How she could leave us. Why'd she go?
Everything seemed together so perfectly.
Full of love, happiness, just to be free.

To leave us here all alone.
To go out, everywhere to roam.
She told me of the boredom life.
She was tired of being another, a wife.

All year long, we showed her the need
To be with us. Who did this awful deed?
Now on the outside looking in
Never to be a part of us, never again.

Bill Wagner

Silence

In our house, there is a silence.
Into our life, it came hence.
Our home was once filled with laughter.
Just being together is all we're after.

This house where love was felt,
A new warmth, this silence will melt.
Our love for each other will grow.
Where it will lead us, we don't know,

Too many nights in this year past,
We thought the silence would last and last.
Our love and laughter will be again
The sunshine of our life to replace the pain.

Today there is a silence only we can explain.
The tears of our hurt, brought about the rain.
Last night with us there was so much strife.
Someone we love, left our life.

I tried really hard to make her see
How much she meant. Why can't it be?
To get her to try with all her might
To have us not spend another silent night.

When Love Dies

I tried, but I didn't realize
To hold on to her, after the love dies.
My love, my pain, my anger I couldn't hide.
Only wanting to be by her side.

I missed her smile, her touch,
To let her know I love her so much.
Now, the love I had is gone.
What we gave her, what we had shown.

She kept telling me she couldn't give
What I needed, my life with her to live
On her we can't depend.
Our love, we'll still send.

She's out there somewhere tonight.
I hope someone's holding her tight.
The love we have her every day,
She didn't want, she walked away.

I tried all year to let her know
It's not what you say, it's what you show.
Hearing I love you gets old.
Feeling the love keeps out the cold.

Bill Wagner

What happens to us, we can't tell.
The love within us will help us heal.
To you, I don't know what we have done
To cause you distance between this one.

The Gift

Last night I heard you cry.
I wanted to comfort you, I wanted to try.
You were so far away from me.
Too far for me to even see.

I asked you what was wrong.
All you said was, "It's gone."
I said, "What have you lost, my dear?"
The bracelet I gave at Christmas, I fear.

Honey, don't cry, don't worry about it.
It's just a bracelet, what it meant
It was from you, you couldn't afford.
I hope I find it, Please help me Lord.

It's the best thing I received all year.
It was like holding him so near.
A gift so very precious to me.
A gift for all the world to see.

I know I'll never find it now.
When or where I lost it, I don't know how.
No one knows what it meant.
A piece of love; Heaven sent.

Bill Wagner

Too Many

Too many nights spent all alone.
Too many nights of what went wrong.
Too much time wondering why.
Too many times, a river to cry.

Too many wasted days of trying.
Feeling too much like I was dying.
Too much time to stop and think.
Too many times I wish I had a drink.

But now all those days are gone.
I'm not living anymore in the twilight zone.
These things I have put behind me.
I try not to remember or let them be.

I can forgive but I can't forget.
What I'm doing now, I hope I don't regret.
I hope that she will understand.
I'm still her friend, I'll hold her hand.

Too many words said, too much shown.
Too many secrets that became unknown.
I didn't want this marriage to end.
All I can be is just her friend.

Why Couldn't I Lie?

Today I did a foolish thing.
I admitted to a fling.
I hurt someone, to me, is very dear.
Now with her, there will be fear.

She was loving me with all her heart.
Now, my deed will keep us apart.
She belongs to another, through a vow.
We wanted to be together, anyhow.

I gave into the desires of the flesh.
In doing so, I created a mess.
The love of a woman who is so sweet
I caused her heart to miss a beat.

I gave her so much pain
She started feeling the rain.
This was the last thing I wanted to do.
To break her heart and make her blue.

To create in her so much doubt.
Her love, I may end up without.
How can I help her mend?
When it was me, the hurt I did send.

Bill Wagner

To me, she could be a wonderful wife.
Someone that would share my life.
Happiness and love, my whole life through
And turn all my gray skies blue.

Tell Me

Tell me, tell me if you can,
What causes a woman to leave a man?
To turn her back on her family.
Oh please, please tell me.

Tell me, tell me, please really try
What to tell my children when they cry.
When they wonder about their mother
Who would rather be with another.

Tell me, tell me, what to say.
Why we're without mother another day.
When they want to run and play.
Why their mother didn't want to stay.

Tell me, tell me, before I die
Why mom didn't try
To make us a family again.
Why she stayed with this man.

Tell me, tell me, please God above
Why mother turned away from our love.
Why we have to suffer with hearts broken?
Why did she leave us for another chosen?

Bill Wagner

Tell me, tell me, did we do anything wrong?
Did we try to hold on too long?
She knows how happy we are to see her.
Why isn't she here? Where is mother?

Precious

Today was as precious as could be
For my love and I were in harmony.
As I laid beside her and felt her touch,
I realized I love her so very much.

I realized why love is so precious
Because someday it could leave us.
When, during time, we take it for granted,
It could leave us, it could be dead.

So precious is each passing day
We need to love in every way.
Not to lie down and make love
But to show love, as God above.

The precious love that we do share
When we show our loved ones we care.
The love we have for our children,
For love of God, for love of man.

The precious love of life
That gets us through this strife.
The love that gets us through the pain
That shields us from the rain.

Bill Wagner

With my world torn apart,
Living with my broken heart,
This precious love of worth untold.
Can someday be mine again to hold?

Jealousy

Jealousy can be such a cruel thing feeling.
It can send your head and heart reeling.
Just because you show a friend you care.
A love you have, apart it will tear.

Telling me things, afraid I'd be mad.
All it did was make my love sad.
Someone told my love a lie.
Now I feel we'll say goodbye.

I couldn't get her to tell me why,
What was wrong, why did she cry.
All she would say, I have more freedom
How she wished that she just had some.

I tried to get her to tell me what's wrong.
She got up and left, she was gone.
She said that she would deal with it.
I just wish I could make her forget.

Someday I'll be able to repair
The place in her heart that has a tear.
Her, I don't want to be without.
Time will erase all the doubt.

Bill Wagner

Without It

A relationship doesn't have a chance.
A love will never last.
A marriage can never continue.
A friendship will be through.

It takes a long time to build strong.
It will be there when things go wrong.
When it's there, it's forever.
Without it, nothing lasts, ever.

It's there in anything you do.
Even when you tie a child's shoe.
It's like love, it has to be built on.
Every day, every way, or it will be gone.

A new love has to learn to trust.
Having friends around you is a must.
Everyone has to understand.
Without it, everything will end.

I Can't Call Your Name

When we're out together, it can't be spoken.
I talk to you without them knowing.
My love for you will go undaunted.
It's like living with a ghost being haunted.

I wish I could tell everyone your name.
For now we have to play the game.
Someday we may have our wish.
Right now, we can't take the risk.

It's sad that we have to slip around
In the dark, back streets in town.
Our friends know we have someone
That is there for us, publicly, no one.

We slip around, steal a kiss.
In your house, my house, us they don't miss.
It's sad that the band of gold
Is just that, the love has grown cold.

To show you attention, he doesn't bother.
Doesn't even suspect that there's another.
If he ever realizes something is wrong,
It will be too late, you'll be gone.

94

Bill Wagner

I wish I could take you in my arms,
Shelter you with love, safe from harm.
I can't call your name, it would be so sweet.
Until that day, we'll sneak around to meet.

She's Afraid

She's afraid of how he will act
When she tells him the fact
Of why she just keeps her distance.
Why she doesn't enjoy his presence.

What has happened while she's alone?
What happened while he stayed gone?
The lonely nights of him not being there.
Passed out in a chair from all the beer.

While he was out doing something other
Than be with her, she found a lover.
Yes, she's afraid of his violent temper,
That he may physically hurt her.

What if he just started to cry?
Could she still tell him good-bye?
She's afraid of being on her own,
Of being with a lover so shortly known.

She's afraid of staying longer.
Maybe he'll give up, just leave her.
She doesn't want to be with him anymore.
Does she have the strength, go out the door?

Bill Wagner

I'm Afraid

I'm afraid he'll do her harm.
I'm afraid he may turn on the charm.
I'm afraid that if he starts to cry
She'll give in to him, won't say good-bye.

I know she says it won't happen.
But I feel somehow, she is saddened.
The dream of what it should have been.
A love grown cold, remember when?

She knows that they deserve better.
I hope he doesn't get angry and hit her.
She talks to them, says she's not happy.
Someday she'll tell them, just maybe.

Sometimes towards him she is so cruel.
It seems like they're in a duel.
He's starting to question what is wrong.
Before you know it, she'll be gone.

I am afraid of what I don't know.
She tells me she loves me. Is it so?
I don't know what the future will hold.
I'm afraid just like him, a love grows cold.

Tomorrow

Awakened from a sleepless night
Wondering if what I'm doing is right.
In a short time it will be gone.
What if this is all wrong?

I still care about her, I know what I feel.
Everything is so scary, it gives me a chill.
I'm not sure if I want to say goodbye.
I don't know if I want to say it's gone. Why?

It felt good when she was here last.
Can I forgive and forget the past?
Can I take the chance it won't happen again?
Can my heart take all the pain?

What if he will return?
What if my heart will burn?
Can I take the chance?
Together can our hearts still dance.

All of this is unknown
Can we make it on our own?
What will happen to us tomorrow?
Will we have happiness or sorrow?

Bill Wagner

She Won't Show

I get so tired of being alone.
A house full of kids but an empty home.
I feel a need to have her by my side.
Not slipping around, trying to hide.

My love for her is so strong.
I know what we do is so wrong.
I want to hold her, keep her warm,
Protect her, keep her safe from harm.

My impatience makes it frustrating.
Our distance apart is what I am hating.
She can't leave, she is not ready.
Our patience is strong, our love is steady.

Tonight, it want to hold her in my arms,
Make love to her, turn on the charm.
I can light her up, make her glow.
But tonight, she won't show.

No Right

I have no right to feel the way I do.
Someone to hold close, to say I love you.
To have in my arms, to say goodnight.
Have her hold me, hold me very tight.

Life has seemed to give me a bad deal.
Complaining won't make it less real.
No right, I have brought this on my own.
These empty feelings, this empty home.

I reach out for someone to hold.
Like the winter's night, it's all too cold.
Make me feel again, is all I ask.
Is this just too hard a task?

It's so hard to remain true.
The touch of a woman, what to do?
No right to force the issue.
My love, I really miss you.

Bill Wagner

Pity

Pity that she walked away
From the home and love, every day.
We talk every now and then
About the way it was, remember when.

Pity I know she doesn't want me to feel
For her, though, is all too real.
Alone, fighting, feeling ignored.
Sitting around, missing home, bored.

Pity she can't tell me what's on her mind.
She can talk to me, I'll be kind.
We talk when she needs a friend.
When he's around, I cannot send.

Pity for a long time I'll be there.
A shoulder to lean on, she knows I care.
We were, through hard times, together.
Time will tell if we'll be there forever.

Why?

I still don't understand why
I miss her sometimes and I sigh.
My love for her she really did hurt.
When I showed her, what's the worth.

This agony that we go through,
Is it necessary what we have to do?
We still long to be one.
The past can't be undone.

The past we can't forget.
I hope this we don't regret.
I still talk of her, of what we had.
When I do, my heart becomes so sad.

She just couldn't say I want to come home.
Now she's out there, humbled inside, alone.
Once in a lifetime you find the love,
A love that could have lasted forever.
The love we just couldn't let be.

Bill Wagner

Too Short

I lost a friend today. So violent
The way it happened, the way he went.
We had just been talking about the strife.
What we had been through, he lost his life.

We worked so close together, my friend.
Who would have ever thought it would end?
To show tomorrow at our workplace.
Not to hear his voice or see his face.

He left two sons he loved so dear.
Now they're alone without him near.
Being with them was all he had.
He's gone now, it's all too sad.

We'll miss him here on this earth,
No one will realize his true worth,
It's very hard to have to report
His love, his friendship, his life too short.

Rollercoaster

When two separate lives are undone,
Emotions go crazy, they get the run-around.
One day you miss them so bad.
The next, you're trying a new fad.

Anything to make the pain go away.
Do what you have to to survive another day.
Wanting to say, bring back the days
When we were crazy in love, all the ways.

When just being with you was such a joy
We'd sit and play with a kid's toy.
Then we remember all the pain.
Do we want to go through this again?

Up and down, around and around, torn apart
It's confusing our mind and our heart.
Why couldn't it be so easy to walk away?
Why can't we find the right words to say?

I love you but I can't show it.
I care, I let you know it.
We're so afraid of what could be,
This rollercoaster ride for you and me.

Bill Wagner

I Hurt Her Again

Can she forgive this imperfect man
Who can't seem to stick to a plan?
To not give her any doubt, just trust.
Give her full devotion, it's a must.

When my ex came around
I gave in, let my guard down.
Gave into a feeling that I thought was gone
Being without her, being on my own.

By doing this, I gave my new love pain.
I didn't think, I hurt her again.
Even though she has someone at home.
He's with her, she's not alone.

No one can even understand
What causes this in a man.
You don't know what's on their mind.
All you realize is you hurt someone kind.

I don't have much to gain.
I just don't want to hurt her again.
She's with her family, I'm alone.
If I'm not careful, she'll be gone.

Alone

Not many understand what it's like to be
Like myself, not having a mate, it's just me.
You go through life, being a pair
Then all of a sudden, one's not there.

The emptiness one feels inside.
Nowhere to run, nowhere to hide.
To loving someone every day, every way.
What do you do? What do you say?

We reach out to share our love,
To give it to anyone on the wings of a dove.
Show someone what it can be
To share this love, a life with me.

I know she doesn't understand.
Will she keep a forgiving hand.
Her love for me has been so sweet.
What she needs, I may not meet.

Being alone can make you so weak,
Giving into a touch, unable to speak,
Not being able to say no.
Not letting true love, have a chance to grow.

Bill Wagner

Two Lives

Two lives so very far apart.
Two lives with each a loving heart.
Two lives who would have known.
Two lives together they have grown.

Two lives they gave each other doubt.
Two lives each other can't do without.
Two lives we gave each other hurt.
Two lives without each other, no worth.

Two lives who fell so deeply in love.
Two lives pray for the blessing from above.
Two lives with each other such a thrill.
Two lives to last an eternity still.

Two lives to endure the pain.
Two lives to share everything.
Two lives a love so hard to hide.
Two lives wanting to be side by side.

Two lives to live it hand in hand.
Two lives with a wall of fears to withstand.
Two lives with a love to last forever.
Two lives who at present, can't be together.

She

"Take me away from all of this," said she.
"Do you want me back, make love to me."
"I don't know," was all I could say.
She messes up my head, confuses me today.

This was her way to say, "Take me back."
Forget the pain to my heart it did attack
The tenderness that we did share
Is this real? Does she care?

I'm afraid to let my guard down.
Afraid of looking like a clown.
A fool in love is what I am.
Can't stand the blows of loneliness, BAM!

Wanting to feel the passion in her touch.
Forgetting about the ghost, loving so much.
Wanting to believe but I can only see.
It's not here that she wants to be.

All the pain and all the strife
Won't let me take back my wife.
All I wanted was an eternity
To spend with this woman. She.

108

Bill Wagner

Take My Hand

So many people who cannot see
What you really mean to me.
We tell everyone that you're just a friend.
On our love, we do depend.

In our heartaches these past few days,
Kept apart but close in so many ways.
Times have been so very hard.
What has happened has left us scarred?

The events have cast some doubt.
Each other, we don't want to be without.
Longing for each other, needing company.
Take my hand, walk with me.

Take my hand, let me share your life.
To be by your side through this strife.
All of this to you is so new.
Take my hand, I'll be true.

With your heart, I need your trust.
To have you near, is such a must.
Wherever we go in this land,
Be by my side, take my hand.

A Love So Scared

Terrified is what I feel.
Being left alone is so real.
My dreams of a future are so dark.
When Cupid shot his arrow, missed the mark

Finding a true love is so very rare.
Committing again, it gives me a scare.
Can I hold on to her? I want to try.
Still wanting someone to hold, I'll ask why.

All my life I've had this dream.
So evasive it does seem.
What does it take to have a love stay?
When the one you love goes away?

Again I would take this chance.
Be with me, can I have this dance?
The love in my heart will be true.
I want to make sure I'm dancing with you.

Yes, I have a love that is scared.
Because I love you, my reputation's smeared
I don't want to cause you pain.
To walk with you in sunshine, not rain.

Bill Wagner

The Rock

Security is what she did need.
It wasn't lust, it wasn't greed.
To have the things she never did.
The real reason it was hid.

The picture, the flowers, the song.
What was to happen, was it so wrong?
To have someone to take care
Of her, what was there to fear?

Reaching out, taking her hand
Walking her through this troubled land.
Needing the love, afraid to let it show.
A painful past, did they know?

Now the guilt is so much to bear.
Sleepless nights, pulling her hair.
The endless sound of a ticking clock.
Why did I take the rock?

It is such a beautiful stone
Sitting in its case, so all alone.
The courage I need, I lack.
I'm not ready, take it back.

111

Looking Good

I saw her today, she looked good.
She smiled at me like she only could.
I talked to her to see if she's okay.
She's doing good, making her way.

All the pain was nowhere in sight.
I gave her a hug, held her tight.
Breaking up is so very hard to do.
All the mixed emotions we must go through.

Being able just to talk means so much.
I'm getting over missing her touch.
Getting over all the hurt and strife.
We're getting on with our life.

The memories will never fade.
The happiness we shared, we made.
I hope she takes care of herself.
Just to knowing her was my wealth.

Bill Wagner

Tough Love

To meet someone who touches your soul:
A wife, a family, a home, was our goal.
Everything we ever wanted, now lost.
The price we paid, what is the cost?

We tried so hard, all in vain.
Got tired of keeping away the rain.
The happiness of our children we share.
One would hurt, the other would care.

Never having what the other would need:
Money, attention, too much greed.
Giving our all was not enough.
Keeping it together made it really tough.

We both tried to end our life.
Couldn't stand any more strife.
Wanting to bring it all to an end
Walking away, trying to be a friend.

Too many years of walking side by side.
Won't try to make it work, so much pride.
A union blessed by God above.
Trying to hold on to a tough love.

This Special Friend of Mine

I very seldom would call her name
Though she's still precious just the same.
I haven't known her but less than a year
But to my heart, she's very dear.

In her life, she felt robbed.
Being a homemaker was her job.
Staying at home, always dependable.
Why was her husband so cruel?

He cheated and lied.
Always there, she tried.
Out on her own, doing her thing.
Now she's learning to give life a fling.

Her eyes light up, her heart does sing.
She doesn't need a wedding ring.
This wonderful life that she's found.
She doesn't need a man around.

With her friends, there's so much fun.
Can't sit still, always on the run.
To me, she doesn't know what it means
That I can call her friend, my friend Darlene.

Bill Wagner

Her Wish

She always wondered if she could
Make a life with this man that understood.
He left her years ago
On the rebound, she still loved him so.

Throughout the years, he crossed her mind.
I loved her, I wasn't unkind.
Thinking he was erased from her past.
She'll be with him, now at last.

What kind of life with him will it be?
Only in time will anyone see.
With him she'll take the chance.
I thank you dear for our dance.

I hope he knows he's a lucky man.
I knew her once, I held her hand.
Will I be the same kind of memory?
I miss her, will she miss me?

Her wish, I hope it comes true.
He doesn't break her heart, make her blue.
It will last if he gives her all.
If he doesn't, it will be a hard fall.

My Doubt

Alone, I'm just pondering.
Back through life, I go wandering
To my childhood where it began
Dealing with the insecurity the best I can.

It seems that throughout this life,
There's always been heartache and strife.
Not being able to let my love show.
But inside me, it did grow.

Not being able to hold on
To a love when it was shown.
Trying too hard to make those proud of me.
Pleasing them, couldn't they see?

I guess my priorities are in the wrong place.
I miss my wife, her beautiful face.
I still wish that with her I could be.
Growing old with her, that's all we'd see.

If my new love know how I feel,
Away from me, her heart would reel.
I hope someday I will know what it will take
To have a true love, a future to make.

Bill Wagner

Walking Away

I guess I was hoping for more.
The way she looked walking in the door.
The feelings I have for her inside.
The feelings I can only now hide.

The way we touched when we're alone
Can never be again, they're gone.
With someone else, she'll walk this land.
He's with her, he's on her hand.

I guess it was a matter of time
Before he could say, she's mine.
I'm really gonna miss her so much.
With her ring, her, I cannot touch.

I wish her all that life can be.
She doesn't know what she meant to me.
The feelings I had that did grow,
I've got to turn loose, let them go.

I know she's doing what is best.
She's found a solution to this mess.
I'll think of her in every way.
I can't have her hand, I'm walking away.

Know Me

You knew me a long time ago
When times were good, when it was slow.
You knew me in times of sadness.
Do you know me after this mess?

I haven't changed all that much.
I'm the man who knew your touch.
Do you know me? I tried to keep you warm.
Do you know me when life's doing harm?

Through troubled times, did you know me?
I held you when your cried, it could only be.
When our children came into our life.
When they hurt us, gave us too much strife.

When you left, something inside was broken
I love you, couldn't be spoken.
When life gave you some pain,
You know me, sheltered you from the rain.

When you said I can't love you anymore.
Maybe, with you, I just got bored.
When life now is too much to bear.
You know me, I'll be there, I still care.

Bill Wagner

Talk to Me

Take the time to hold their hand.
Hold them tight, walk through this land.
Take the time for what it will take.
Every day, true love to make.

When their heart is broken,
It's the touch, not the word spoken.
Hold them tight, not saying a thing.
Show them what love will bring.

Take the time to show everyday
A love that grows in every way.
A friend, a love, a confidant.
Be there, give them what they want.

By their side, always be,
Your love for them, let everyone see.
I'll be yours and you'll be mine.
If we'll only take the time.

A Memory

Today I went over the memories
Of what we had, what used to be.
I walked down the lonely old road
Of the tears and fears untold.

Of the time we were on the edge
Where the pain drove us apart like a wedge.
To try to hold on with all my might.
But having another lonely sleepless night.

The times of staying up until dawn,
Walking the floor, hoping she'll come home.
Trying so hard to make everything right.
Knowing she would be leaving tonight.

Are we any better now, like way back when?
Have we learned of what it could've been?
In so many ways we are better.
It's still the same, I'm without her.

When I see her, I want to hold her so bad.
I won't let myself, it's so sad.
I just try to be alone and a friend.
I really care for her, I will till time does end.

Bill Wagner

What Can It Be?

What is it when the feelings are so strong?
When you touch someone, is it wrong?
The oneness we share when we're together.
How can we say we love another.

The fear of what it could be.
Afraid of a future that we can't see.
When we lie together, such a peace unfolds.
The words come so easily, feelings untold.

A closeness that's so hard to explain.
It's puzzling just the same.
What we feel we can't say in a word.
What we're afraid to say, can't be heard.

We say there's someone else in our life
But we turn to each other during strife.
When we need someone to hold us tight,
We call on each other, make it tonight.

The pleasure to each other that we bring.
What we have is a very special thing.
So, why do we try to stay away?
Can't we just let it happen, come what may?

It's a Mind Game

About the Author

Bill has written a few books. Three devotions and a mini biography. He never knew he had a love of writing. It only showed when he was going through changes in his life. There are so many emotions we deal with in life and sometimes, it is best to just write what you are feeling. Don't worry if it upsets someone, it's the relief that you will find that you need.

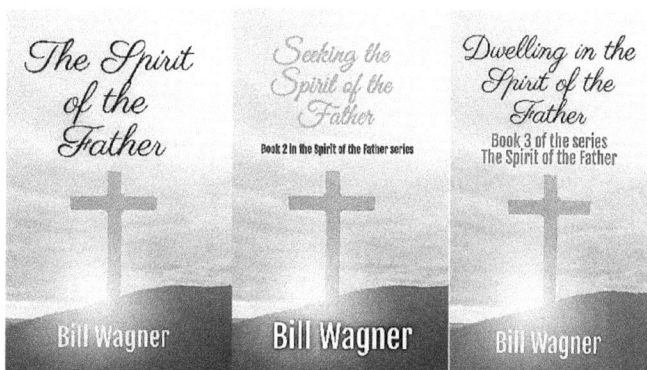

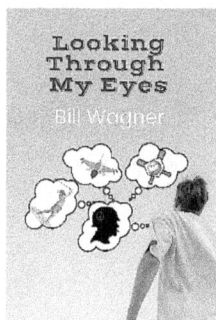

www.ingramcontent.com/pod-product-compliance
Lightning Source LLC
Chambersburg PA
CBHW060113050426
42448CB00010B/1855